Fashion and Clothes

Jack Harvey

Macdonald Educational

Editor Anne Furniss
Design Peter Benoist
Production Philip Hughes
Picture Research Lorna Collin

First published 1975
Macdonald Educational
49 Poland Street
London W1A 2LG

contents

ISBN 0 356 05091 2

© Macdonald & Co.
(Publishers) Limited 1975
Printed and bound by
New Interlitho, Milan, Italy.

Why wear clothes?

The first clothes

Man is born naked. But 100,000 years ago hunters in the Northern Hemisphere made clothes from the skins of wild animals. They also made necklaces and bracelets from their bones. Clothing protected them against bad weather and made it possible for them to hunt when they would otherwise have had to look for shelter. It also made them feel more important and attractive.

No other animal speaks or wears clothes. Man might still be speechless and naked if he had not learnt to make tools. A group or race of men is held together by its common language. In the same way, local materials and styles of dress and decoration help to unite the individuals who share them.

The origins of fashion

Because the first clothes were made from the skins of hunted animals, the importance of the successful hunter increased. Like the tycoon of today he wore the best skins or could share them with his friends. This brought rivalry into fashion, but people did not want to look too unlike one another. Wealth and rank are more often shown by more jewels and better clothes than by clothes of a different type.

Once people start to wear clothes they begin to feel that it is wrong to uncover certain areas of the body. This modesty varies in different times and places. But man first decorated his body because he was proud of it, not because he was afraid of it.

Flint scraper and bone needle

▲ Early man skinned the animals he killed with a flint scraper like this one. He then softened the skins by biting them, as Eskimo women still do. A splinter of bone was used as a needle and animal gut made thread for the first sewing.

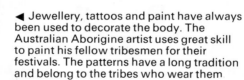

◄ Jewellery, tattoos and paint have always been used to decorate the body. The Australian Aborigine artist uses great skill to paint his fellow tribesmen for their festivals. The patterns have a long tradition and belong to the tribes who wear them

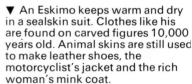

▼ An Eskimo keeps warm and dry in a sealskin suit. Clothes like his are found on carved figures 10,000 years old. Animal skins are still used to make leather shoes, the motorcyclist's jacket and the rich woman's mink coat.

The first materials natural fibres

Woven fabrics

Clothes are made from four main sorts of natural fibres: wool, silk, cotton and flax. One of the most important developments in man's history occurred when he first saw the possibility of spinning short fibres together and weaving them into cloth. He became a farmer and herdsman as well as a hunter of wild animals.

Sheep were herded in Central Asia in prehistoric times. An inscription dated 4200B.C. describes the work of weavers and dyers in Mesopotamia. Felt was the earliest wool cloth. To make it, the fleece is shorn from the sheep and pounded together with water till it mats into a warm, stiff fabric. More than half the world's wool is now produced in Australia.

A closely guarded secret

Cotton comes from the seed-head of a semi-tropical plant. The earliest spun cotton yarn was found in the ruins of Mohenjo-Daro in Pakistan and is 3,000 years old. Today, the largest growers are the U.S., U.S.S.R. and China.

Linen fibres come from the stem of an annual plant called flax. The fibres are freed by rotting the stems in water, a process known as retting.

For 2,000 years the secrets of silk-worm cultivation were known only to the Chinese. Silk togas imported by the Romans cost their own weight in gold. But in the sixth century two Persian monks smuggled some cocoons out of China in their hollow walking sticks and brought the skill to Byzantium. From there it spread to Europe.

▼ The symbols on this map show the main production areas of natural fibres today. The lines linking the pictures to the map show where the fibres were first produced. Sheep's wool has been used to make cloth for so long that its origins are lost in history.

Key to modern production areas
- ▲ *Wool*
- △ *Cotton*
- ● *Silk*
- ○ *Flax*
- ★ *Mohair*
- ☆ *Alpaca, llama, vicuna etc.*
- ◆ *Cashmere*

▲ These women in Peru wear blankets and skirts made of wool. In the Andes wool is taken from llamas as well as sheep, and two other animals of the llama family, the alpaca and the vicuna, are bred for their very fine hair. It is made into the finest quality suits and coats. Wool blankets and ponchos have been worn in South America for thousands of years.

▶ This 3,000-year old Egyptian tomb painting shows Queen Nefertari in a finely woven linen dress. This lightweight fabric was ideal for the hot climate of Egypt, and flax grew easily along the banks of the River Nile. The goddess on her right wears a dress made from coloured beads. Now, most of the world's flax is grown in the U.S.S.R. and central Europe.

How silk is produced

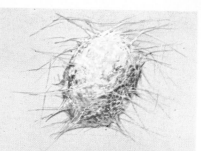

▲ The female silk moth cannot fly and only lives for a few days. But she lays more than 500 eggs during this time.

▲ The larva feeds only on the leaves of the mulberry tree. During its eight weeks of life it sheds its skin three times.

▲ The larva takes five days to make its cocoon. The silk is spun from two sticky fluids which combine to make a single thread.

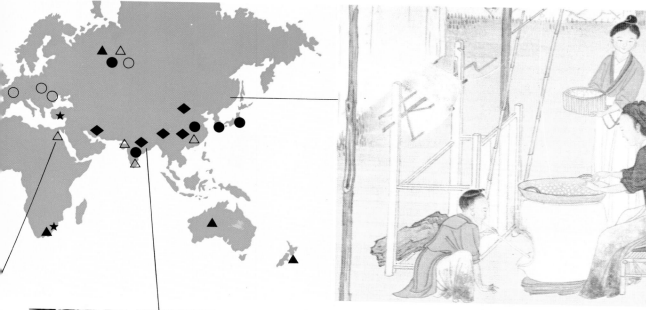

▲ This Chinese painting shows silk being collected from cocoons in a basket. Two or three strands of silk are wound off together to give the yarn strength. The women doing the work are themselves wearing silk dresses. For centuries it was the only fibre used in China. China and Japan are still major silk producers.

◀ The women in this Indian market are wearing cotton saris. The rich prefer silk and today synthetic fabrics are often used. But cotton was first spun in the Indian sub-continent. Until the 18th century Europeans could only weave a coarse cotton and linen mixture called fustian. Indian weavers could produce a very fine cloth called muslin, which was highly prized in Europe.

5

From fibre to fabric hand made clothes

These scenes show all the processes involved in making woollen cloth for the simple clothes of the Middle Ages. They have been copied from miniature paintings in mediaeval books, from which we have obtained much of our information about the period.

Chitons and togas

To make a piece of cloth by hand is a very slow process. Early clothes were often made from one piece of material, without any cutting, so as to avoid waste. The Greek chiton and Roman toga were basically lengths of cloth wound around the body. They were pinned and tied and sometimes had sleeves, but there was no tailoring to fit the body.

Certain colour dyes were rare in classical times. Roman purple came from cuttle fish and was imported from Crete and Tyre. It was considered so valuable that only senators were allowed to wear it. A single purple band decorated their plain togas.

The Middle Ages

The structure of clothes varied very little from Greek and Roman times until the 14th century. By then, garments were often fastened with thongs like shoe laces and buttons were very popular.

Fashion in the modern sense began at the court of the Dukes of Burgundy and in Northern Italy. Florence was an important centre for the dyeing and weaving of luxury woollen cloth. Lucca and Venice produced silk and Genoa was famous for its velvet. The clothes of the rich became increasingly elaborate, but until the 18th century every bit of cloth was spun, woven and sewn by hand.

► Shearing
The sheep shears used in the 15th century had not changed in 2,000 years. The fleece was removed in one piece and it took great skill to remove it neatly without nicking the animal.

► Carding
This process prepared the wool for spinning. A small quantity of wool at a time was pulled between two spiked boards until it was free from tangles. For finer yarns a comb with longer prongs was used.

◄ Weaving
The first stage of weaving is to tie long threads parallel to each other between two beams. These are called warp threads. Then another thread, called the weft, is drawn from side to side passing under and over alternate warps. The weft is held in a shuttle. The heddle lifts the warps to form a path through which the shuttle flies.

► Dyeing
Two substances are required for dyeing. One produces the colour and one fixes the colour in the cloth. The fixing substance is known as the mordant. Plants and the bark of trees provided many of the colours. Alum, salt and urine were used as mordants.

◄ The chiton was worn by both sexes in ancient Greece. All Greek clothes were based on simple rectangles of cloth draped and then pinned at the shoulder. A girdle was the only other fastening. These flowing draperies were made of wool or linen and would fit anyone. For over 1,000 years, clothes continued to be based on this pattern and were untailored with simple fastenings.

► The German lancer of 1530 wore clothes cut in a style far more complicated than anything seen earlier. The arms and legs were slashed so as to show off the coloured lining. This military fashion of slashing was adopted by courtiers of both sexes and lasted nearly 200 years.

Spinning

Spinning by hand is very slow and requires great patience. The object is to twist the fibres and draw them out so that they form a continuous strong thread. In the older method the wool is on the top of the distaff and is spun, or twisted, by hand onto the spindle below.

The speed of spinning was greatly accelerated by the invention of the spinning wheel. It first came into use in Europe in the 13th century and still had to be turned by hand. Eventually it was fitted with a treadle, leaving both the spinster's hands free.

▲ **Fulling**
The next stage was to give the woven cloth body. The cloth was trampled in a tub of fuller's earth, a substance which felts fibres to an even texture.

▲ **Napping and cropping**
The surface of the cloth was then raised, or napped, by brushing with the prickly head of the teazel plant. Cropping shears then trimmed it to a uniform pile.

▲ **Tailor's shop**
The mediaeval tailor made clothes to order for wealthy customers. Only hats and hosiery were sold ready-made. His equipment included a yardstick for measuring the cloth.

The love of luxury

▲ On this jewel from the tomb of Tutankhamun the ancient Egyptian God Horus is shown as a hawk. The stone on the god's head represents the rising sun. The devices on top of his claws are ankhs, symbols of life which express the hope that the young king will rise from the dead. Gold, lapis lazuli and hundreds of pieces of glass form the outstretched wings.

▼ Queen Elizabeth I used her appearance as a weapon of state. She ruled England at a time of great uncertainty. It was important that the country should present a united face to the world. Her elaborate clothes, jewels, wigs and make-up made her seem a strong, rich monarch.

Spiritual protection

Decorating the body fulfils a basic human need. Even primitive people find time to develop the skills of making jewellery. In many societies a huge proportion of energy and wealth is devoted to decking the body with beautiful but unnecessary objects. One motive for this effort can be religion or superstition. A Star of David or a cross is worn round the neck to give spiritual protection to the wearer. For the same reason, some American Indians made necklaces from the fingers of the enemies they killed.

Local materials

The kind of decoration worn often depends on the materials that are available. In South America, brilliantly coloured capes and ponchos used to be woven from the feathers of native birds. On the East coast of Africa and elsewhere jewellery is made from shells.

Some shells, such as the cowrie, are used as money. The cowrie shell has also been a fertility charm since prehistoric times.

Precious stones

Some stones and metals are valuable because they are rare. Wearing them increases the owner's status. But the ancient Egyptians and the Elizabethans were happy to use precious stones and coloured glass together.

The Elizabethans loved pearls for brooches, necklaces and earrings. They also stitched them onto doublets and dresses to add to the richness of the fabric. Many Italian portraits of the 15th century show strings of pearls entwined in a young lady's golden hair. They were said to have magic powers.

The mystery of gold

Gold has always been highly valued. It is very heavy and its lustre is not spoiled by rust or corrosion like other metals. Its softness makes it easy to work. Kings and great priests have often worn cloth of gold, which is material with thin strands of gold woven into it.

Christian wedding rings have been plain gold since the 13th century. At first they were worn on the right hand fingers or even the thumb. Now, they are always worn on the third finger of the left hand.

Lace

Lace was a very fashionable form of decoration in the 17th and 18th centuries and was worn by anyone who could afford it. It seems to have reached Europe via Cyprus and Venice.

▲ *Point de Venise,* or *Gros Point,* is worked with a needle. It gives a high relief effect almost like sculpture. Most of the cuffs and cravats of the late 17th century were of *Gros Point.* They cost about £50 each.

▲ Bobbin lace is usually lighter in style than needlepoint lace. This piece was made in Flanders, where lace-making was a major industry by the 16th century. All girls over the age of five learned the craft so that they could be self-supporting by the age of ten.

▲ A prosperous middle class couple in 17th century Holland. No expense has been spared on their clothes. The cut of her dress wastes yards of costly material and even his boots are topped with lace. The cane and gloves were high fashion at the time and so were the braiding and decorative rosettes.

How bobbin lace is made

Bobbin lace is made on a special pillow with each of the dozens of separate linen threads hanging down on their bobbins when not in use. They are worked around one another and kept in place by pins at the centre. These brass pins were costly and the poor often made do with thorns. Lace is only expensive because of the time and skill needed to make it. In the 1860s, 36 workers spent 18 months making a lace dress for the Empress Eugénie of France.

◄ The pattern of the lace is pricked out at the centre of the pillow. The weight of the bobbins keeps them free.

► The threads are wound on these bobbins. Bobbins carved from bone with glass spangles were often family heirlooms.

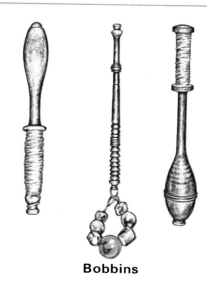

Bobbins

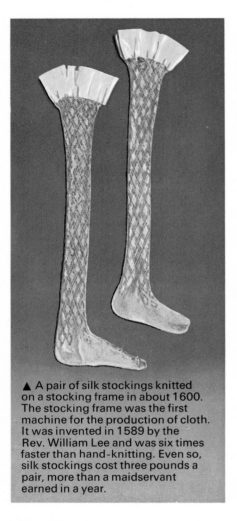

▲ A pair of silk stockings knitted on a stocking frame in about 1600. The stocking frame was the first machine for the production of cloth. It was invented in 1589 by the Rev. William Lee and was six times faster than hand-knitting. Even so, silk stockings cost three pounds a pair, more than a maidservant earned in a year.

▼ John Kay's flying shuttle was the start of the mechanical revolution in clothmaking. It enabled the weaver to flick the shuttle containing the weft thread from side to side without moving from his position at the centre of the loom. A hand-held rod was connected by cords to sliders at each side. It made weaving faster and it was no longer necessary to employ two men on broad widths of cloth. John Kay made no money from his invention and died in poverty in 1781.

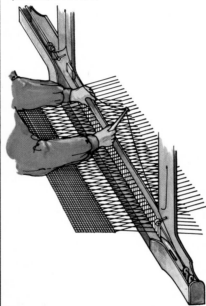

The Industrial Revolution

In the last half of the 18th century the production of cloth was completely revolutionized. This was brought about by the invention in quick succession of machines to handle all the stages of production from carding to weaving.

The invention which made all the others necessary was the flying shuttle. It enabled weavers to work so much faster that it caused a shortage of yarn. But it was not until 1768, 30 years later, that Richard Arkwright patented his water frame. This was the first effective mechanical spinner.

Arkwright opened a mill in Nottingham and then a larger mill at Cromford. There his machines were powered by the water of the Derwent. To make his yarns stronger and more even in thickness he developed the drawer frame. It extended the fibres and gave them a twist before spinning.

These mills were among the first modern factories. Soon, people found they could no longer make a living spinning by hand in their own homes. There were riots and two of Arkwright's mills were burnt down. To prevent it happening again he installed cannons and armed his loyal workers.

Automatic machinery

In 1786, Dr Cartwright patented a power-driven loom and in 1804, Jacquard's device for weaving patterned cloth appeared. By 1900 there were looms which could feed themselves with new bobbins of weft thread and stop automatically when faults occurred. It took two men to operate a wide hand loom. Now one weaver can superintend two dozen or more machines.

Because of these new machines, cotton was produced in such large quantities by the 1820s that it was very cheap. The poor could no longer afford the warm woollen clothes worn by earlier generations. Instead they wore cotton.

◀ A mill scene in the 1830s. Within a few years of the invention of Arkwright's water frame, mills were built with dozens and then hundreds of machines driven by one source of power. Women and children were employed because they were cheap. On the left the cotton is being carded and on the right it is being made ready for spinning.

Sewing machine stitches

Sewing machines do not use the same sort of stitches that are used in hand-sewing. Continuous thread is used and the needle can only travel up and down, not under and over.

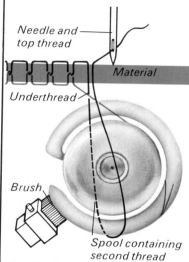

Needle and top thread

Material

Underthread

Brush

Spool containing second thread

Lock stitch

▲ A lock stitch machine uses two spools of thread. The top thread is moved down by the needle. The underthread is fed from a disc-shaped bobbin. The two interlock when the first is carried below the bobbin by the revolving hook. The bobbin thread then passes through the loop. The hook is slowed down by a brush to make the last stitch tight.

Chain stitch

▲ Single thread chain stitch. Below the cloth is a device to make a loop in the first stitch. The next stitch is made in the middle of the loop, so each stitch is held by the one before.

▶ Modern knitted materials are designed with the help of a computer. The information is fed in through the tele-type keyboard. An electronic scanner traces small areas of the pattern and enlarges them on the television monitor. The designer can see the effect of the finished fabric at once.

An early Singer sewing machine

▼ The sewing machine caused a revolution in the making of clothes. Until its invention around 1850, every stitch of clothing had been sewn by hand.
This machine makes a lock stitch. The handle on the right turns a main shaft which is geared to drive the needle and shuttle. Four million copies of this Singer model were sold all over the world in 20 years from 1865.

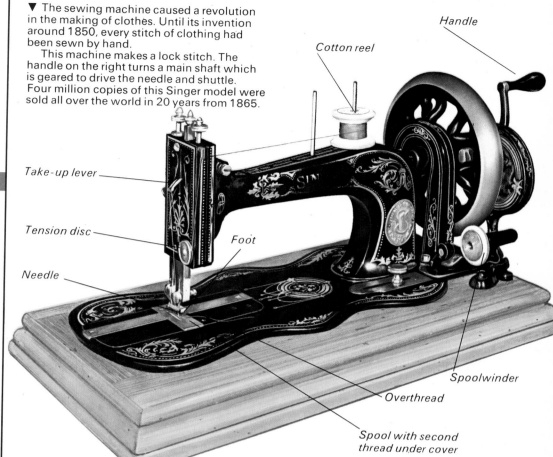

Handle

Cotton reel

Take-up lever

Tension disc

Foot

Needle

Spoolwinder

Overthread

Spool with second thread under cover

White cotton, black slaves

▲ The fluffy white boll which follows the flower on the cotton plant brought great wealth to some and misery to millions of others. In the U.S. most plantations grew Sea Island cotton which has a long staple fibre, suitable for machine spinning.

The slave trade triangle

The spinning machines of the 18th century needed new supplies of cotton. Most of it was grown in the southern states of the U.S. To make the crop profitable, a large cheap labour force was needed to pick and clean the cotton. So the planters bought African slaves. There were already slaves on sugar and tobacco plantations, but in the 20 years before 1800 the population doubled to one million. Almost all the increase was due to cotton.

Britain banned the slave trade in 1807, but until then many of the ships which carried human cargoes belonged to Liverpool ship owners. They exported cheap printed calico to West Africa, where the cloth was traded for slaves. The ships then sailed for Charleston and New Orleans. There the slaves were sold by auction and the new cotton crop bought for use in the Lancashire mills.

Human cargoes

Each ship carried more than 600 slaves packed together with only 1.8 m. (6 ft) by 0.3 m. (1 ft) of floor space each. In places the ceiling was only 0.8 m. high ($2\frac{1}{2}$ ft). Sometimes as many as a quarter of the Africans died on the Atlantic crossing, which could take as long as 20 weeks.

Planters stood to make more money from healthy contented slaves, so most of them probably treated their slaves no worse than their other servants. But there was also great cruelty. An average day's pick in the cottonfields was 22.7 kg. (50 lbs.). One Mississippi overseer, armed with a whip, made his men pick 136 kg. (300 lbs.) a day each.

As a result of this trade more cotton became available and ladies could buy fine muslin dresses much more cheaply. By 1800 the price of muslin had dropped from one pound a yard to five shillings (25p) or even less.

A mid-19th century American cotton plantation

◀ Free millworkers in England often lived in worse conditions than slaves. In the 50 years up to 1830 Manchester quadrupled in population because of cotton. Overcrowded slums led to disease and the river was black with pollution from the dye-houses.

▲ In 1793 Eli Whitney invented a machine called a gin for separating the seeds from the cotton boll. This gin was 50 times faster than hand cleaning. A steam gin was 1,000 times faster.

▼ A paddle-steamer waits to be loaded with the new crop. The use of steam powered ships cut the cost of the Atlantic crossing. But the price of slaves went on rising until the Civil War ended slavery in 1862.

▼ The cotton was ginned and baled on the plantation before being sent to the Lancashire mills. By 1840 there were two million slaves on cotton plantations. They made up almost a quarter of the population of the U.S.

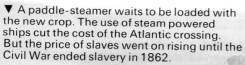

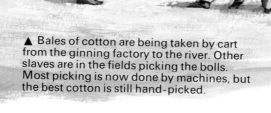

▲ Bales of cotton are being taken by cart from the ginning factory to the river. Other slaves are in the fields picking the bolls. Most picking is now done by machines, but the best cotton is still hand-picked.

The changing shape of beauty

► In 1856 steel hoops were invented to replace the horse hair padding of early crinolines. Cartoons such as this mocked the new fashion. But the joke depended on the fact that Victorian men found the glimpse of a woman's ankle very exciting.

▼ In the last 200 years each generation has had its own ideal shape for a woman. These shapes have reflected man's view of her. In 1770 she was straight-laced and aloof. In 1802 she wore no corsets and talked of equality. In the crinoline she was a fragile doll, in the S-bend a temptress. Perhaps real equality will force more women to wear trousers.

1770
Hooped paniers

1803
Empire line muslin dress

1830
Leg of mutton sleeves

1865
Crinoline

1884
Bustle

Why follow fashion?

Man's idea of what is beautiful is always changing and new fashions help women to add to their attractions. Men have often laughed at the extreme styles. But they have always shown interest in the woman whose clothes drew attention to new areas of her body. This can be done by padding, by wearing tight corsets or by exposing some area of the body. Sometimes the three are used together.

Many wide crinoline dresses left the shoulders bare. The new V-neckline of 1913 was considered quite shocking. In the 1920s the knees were revealed and ten years later there were backless evening gowns. But bare flesh in fashion must have reached its limits with the micro-skirts and see-through blouses of the late 1960s.

Every fashion goes through three phases. At first it is surprising and even shocking. Then it is popular. When it becomes too popular it loses its charm and a new fashion emerges.

Whalebone and laces

Corsets usually got their strength from strips of whalebone. This made possible both the stiff tapered torso of 1770 and the S-bend of 1900. The tiny waists of the 1830s were the result of the merciless tightening of laces at the back. Full sleeves and skirts with voluminous petticoats added to the effect.

Fashions for rich and poor

Most portraits painted before the invention of the camera show a small wealthy class of society in their best clothes. Like today's fashion pictures they tell us mainly how people would have liked to look. The extremes of fashion could only be worn by the rich.

Popular styles which lasted some time, such as the crinoline and the bustle, were worn even by servants and factory girls. One housemaid is said to have faked a bustle by stuffing three dusters under her skirt. Country people often wore styles that had long ago lost favour in the big cities.

▲ The corset of the 1920s was made of a new elasticated material. Instead of drawing attention to breasts and hips it gave a woman a flat tubular look.

1902
S-bend

1913
Hobble

1928
Short evening dress

1930
Backless evening dress

1948
Dior's "New Look"

1968
Mini-skirt

False hair and painted faces

▲ The warrior kings of ancient Assyria had their hair and beards elaborately curled. Like Samson, their long hair gave them male strength.

▲ Roman men had short hair at the time of the Republic. They were also clean shaven and even plucked their chests.

▲ Long wigs were replaced by short white-powdered ones in the 18th century. Church and legal leaders wore wigs long after the fashion died and so did the servants of the nobility.

▲ This modern toupé hides baldness, which many men fear makes them less attractive. Hair weaving and transplanting can also be used to disguise a lack of hair.

Religion and the head

The head is the most important part of the body. This is made clear by the number of religious customs relating to it.

The Sikhs of India are not allowed to cut their hair or trim their beards; Buddhist monks shave their heads. Orthodox Jewish men must wear a hat or skull cap and for prayer they also cover their heads with a shawl. In Christian churches men remove their hats. Every one of these gestures is a sign of respect, yet each society interprets them differently.

A woman's crowning glory

In the Middle Ages a woman's hair was thought to be so seductive that it was permanently veiled. The devout Jewish woman used to cover her hair with a wig so that only her husband ever saw her real beauty.

Wigs have usually been worn to follow a fashion and natural-looking hair has seldom been popular. In ancient Egypt even the poor wore wigs. They could not afford human hair so they used flax.

The face and fashion

In the 16th century, freckles were loathed and feared because they reminded people of smallpox scars, so women hid them under thick layers of rice and flour powder. Only a generation or two later there was a fashion for sticking velvet patches on the face for the same reason. The patches were cut in circles or shaped like hearts or flowers.

A dark complexion has always been despised because the peasants were sun tanned. But from 1930 onwards everyone wanted to look bronzed. It was a sign of being wealthy enough to spend the winter in a warm climate.

Showing off with a hat

Hats are a very easy way of showing off wealth and status. The practical hoods and veils of the Middle Ages were replaced in the 15th century by hats of all shapes and sizes. French court ladies wore the hennin, a hat like a church steeple. In Flanders there were gauze creations held out by wire to make butterfly wings on either side of the head. Their size and elegance made it clear that these women did no work.

▲ This young Florentine lady has had the fashionable beauty treatment of 1465. Her hairline and eyebrows have been plucked to make her forehead into a broad dome. The hair itself has been dyed blonde as it often was in Roman times.

▲ A cartoon of 1776 mocks the size and elaboration of the hairstyles then in fashion. False hair and cloth pads were used to increase the height. Ships and stuffed birds were used for decoration but this lady carries her entire dressing-table.

Modern beauty treatment

The "Afro" hairdo became popular as black people stopped trying to copy white ideals of beauty. It was even used as a basis for wigs in non-Afro colours. Like men's wigs in the 18th century, there is no attempt to imitate natural hair.

False eyelashes, eye-shadow and a pencilled eyebrow all make the eye seem larger and brighter. In Asia surgeons have made fortunes operating on women to give them the eye shape typical of European women.

Nose shapes vary in fashion as much as any part of the face. Modern surgery can make a woman's nose longer, shorter, thinner or thicker. The "face-lift" operation stretches her skin to remove wrinkles.

For centuries European women craved a white skin. They used white lead, which is a poison. They also used egg-white. Pink was added to the cheeks for a youthful bloom. Each year now gives the face a new fashion colour.

Only since the 1920s has it been thought respectable for a woman to colour her lips. Fashions in lipstick have varied from almost natural pale shades to very shiny brilliant reds. Few lipsticks pretend to be natural.

◀ This cosmetics box belonged to an Egyptian woman in 1300 B.C. She used a strongly stylised eye make-up including green malachite on the lids. Many of the oils and colours are still used today.

▶ The modern cosmetics industry produces lotions and creams to clean and restore the skin, as well as make-up to disguise it. Scent, colour and packaging add glamour to products largely made from oils and waxes. Advertising encourages the belief that beauty can be found in a jar or tube.

17

Clothes and the scientist

The fibre revolution

Until the end of the last century all clothes were made either from the hair or skin of animals or from vegetable fibres like cotton and flax, which could easily be spun.

In 1883, Sir Joseph Wilson Swan was trying to perfect the filament for an electric light bulb. He succeeded in forcing a nitrocellulose solution through a jet so that it hardened into a long strand, and so discovered a process for making artificial fibres.

At the 1889 Paris exhibition there was a display of fabrics produced by a similar French process. By the 1930s this artificial silk, called rayon, was very popular and in great demand for women's underwear and nightdresses.

New materials

Nylon was the first purely synthetic yarn to be used for textiles. It was invented in the U.S. by Wallace H. Carothers. Unlike rayon it is produced by an entirely chemical process. The modern wide range of synthetic yarns is mainly made from by-products of petrol refining.

Clothes made from synthetic fibres are easy to wash and quick to dry as they absorb less moisture and dirt than fabrics made from natural fibres. It is now possible for the whole family to dress in clothes that need no ironing.

Aniline dyes, made from a highly poisonous by-product of coal, were discovered in 1836. Vegetable dyes are now no longer used commercially as chemical dyes are cheaper and last longer.

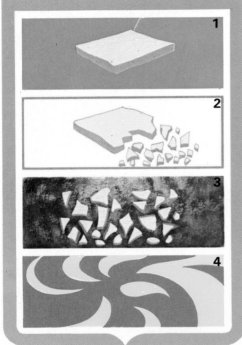

How rayon is made

Cellulose is the basic ingredient of rayon and is found in all forms of plant life. The high grade cellulose used to make rayon comes from the pulp of Canadian Spruce and South African Eucalyptus trees. The cellulose is extracted at the pulp mills, then pressed and cut into sheets.

1. At the rayon factory, the cellulose must be dissolved and turned into a liquid chemical substance so that it can be spun. The first stage is to immerse the cellulose in caustic soda, which combines with it to produce alkali cellulose.

2. The alkali cellulose is broken into crumbs.

3. The alkali cellulose is stored to allow oxygen in the air to oxydize it. This reduces the molecular size.

4. The alkali cellulose is mixed with a chemical called carbon disulphide to form sodium cellulose xanthate.

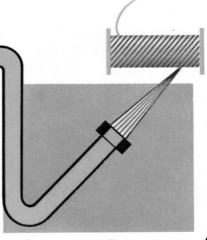

◄ When dissolved in caustic soda, the sodium cellulose xanthate becomes a syrupy solution called viscose. The viscose is allowed to "ripen" and air bubbles and solid particles are removed.

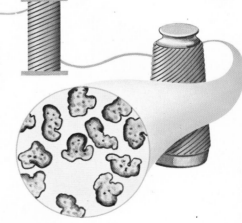

▲ The viscose is forced through holes in a narrow jet into a tank of sulphuric acid. This causes it to solidify as a continuous thread, which is stretched and wound onto a reel. Then the yarn is washed and dried before being twisted onto a bobbin. It is now ready to be woven or knitted.

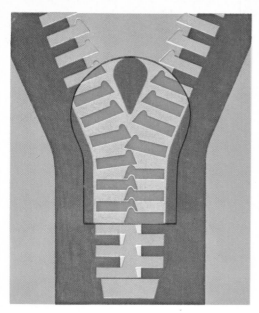

20th century fastenings

◀ The slide fastener, usually known as the zip, is another 20th century invention. It was first mass produced in the U.S. just before World War I. Long rows of buttons or hooks and eyes are now no longer necessary. The slider angles each individual tooth outwards and upwards so that the tooth opposite can fasten into the notch on its underside. The teeth on a nylon zip are a different shape but the locking principle is the same.

▶ Velcro is a more recent invention than the zip and is a scientific development of the hook and eye. But it requires no skill or effort to operate. When the very fine nylon loops on the left are pressed onto the hooks on the right they automatically lock themselves on. Unfastening is simply a matter of tugging the two halves apart.

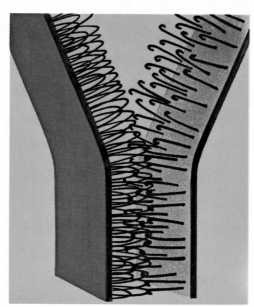

▼ All the clothes in this scene are synthetic, even the shoes and zips. Many fabrics are designed to look like textiles of natural origin and man-made leather and fur are hard to tell from the real thing. But the girl's P.V.C. coat is in a style as new as the material used to make it.

Sold by the million mass production

Most clothes nowadays are sold by chain stores with branches in all large towns. One company sells £500 million worth of clothes a year through 251 stores. They employ a design staff and scientists to develop new dyes and fabrics. But they have the clothes manufactured by independent firms.

▶ The first stage in the production of mass-produced clothes. A mechanized knife cuts several dozen layers of cloth at a time. It is the most important invention for the fast production of clothes since the sewing machine. Previously each piece had to be cut out separately, but now far fewer skilled cutters are needed.

Cutting out

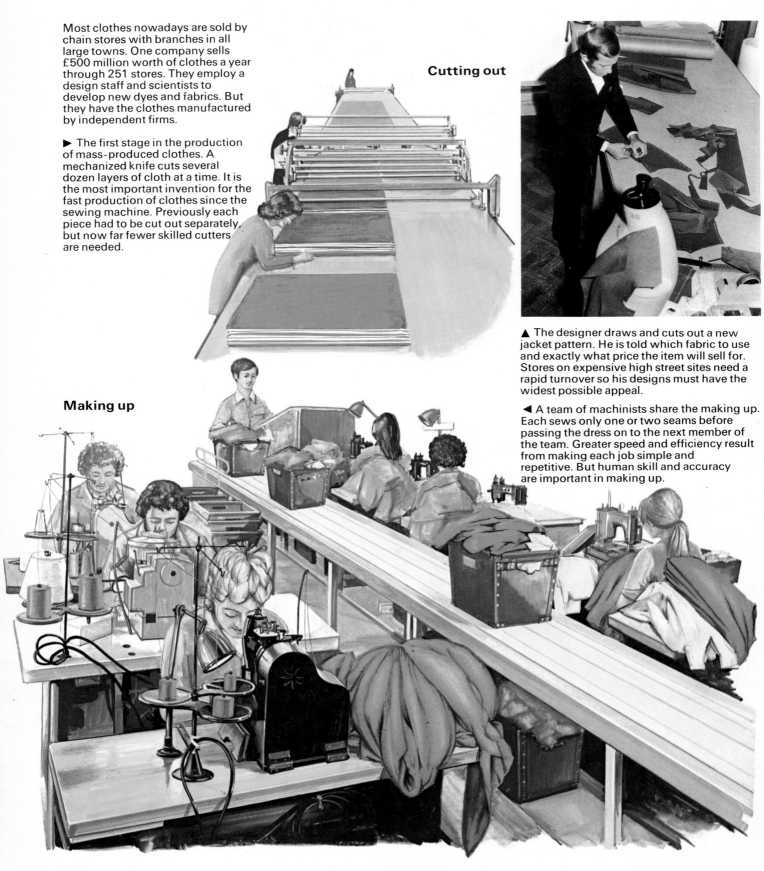

▲ The designer draws and cuts out a new jacket pattern. He is told which fabric to use and exactly what price the item will sell for. Stores on expensive high street sites need a rapid turnover so his designs must have the widest possible appeal.

◀ A team of machinists share the making up. Each sews only one or two seams before passing the dress on to the next member of the team. Greater speed and efficiency result from making each job simple and repetitive. But human skill and accuracy are important in making up.

Making up

◄ A special machine is used to make collars and cuffs. The machinist is being watched by supervisors who are responsible for the smooth running of the factory. The designer's instructions even cover the type of button or other fastenings which will be used.

▼ Pieces of the dress are ironed before being put together. A new line is first made in a small sample quantity. Any snags which affect the cost or finish may lead to its being re-designed before mass production.

Pressing

Examining

▲ The finished clothes are checked both lying flat and hanging up. It is important that every garment is correctly sized and of good quality. In mass production a single fault can spread to hundreds of garments. And a chain store must keep its reputation for reliability

▲ A new dress is photographed for a newspaper fashion page. Chain stores do not create fashion but to some extent they follow it. They aim to sell tens of thousands of copies of a dress. So they limit the range of colours and sizes to avoid extremes of style.

Whatever happened to national costume?

▲ All the delegates at the United Nations are dressed the same. At one time a gathering of the world's leaders would have been full of colour and variety. The rows of sober suits indicate that all countries now face similar economic and social conditions.

▶ In Volendam in Holland the old local costume is still worn to attract the tourists. The starched lace cap used to be kept for Sundays. Coral necklaces with a different number of strands are worn in other villages.

▼ The traditional Maori costume is made of flax leaves. Cloaks and kilts made from this local plant were the only clothes before Europeans arrived in New Zealand. Now they are worn only on festive occasions.

▲ The Hunza live in the mountains between Pakistan and China. Being so far from modern cities they still wear traditional clothes. The pillbox hat is decorated with typical geometric embroidery.

Vanishing skills

National costume is fast disappearing. A century ago each isolated community in Europe had its own local costume. These costumes now only appear on special occasions or to attract tourists. People are more at ease in jeans or drip-dry clothes.

Since 1900 much has happened to iron out the differences between living in one place or another. Television and magazines spread new fashions around the world. Central heating has made climate less important. People with cars walk less. When they do walk, the roads are paved and without the puddles and mud which made clogs useful.

Cheap, mass produced clothes have resulted in far less local spinning and weaving, and modern methods of farming have sent more people into the cities. Once there, they no longer have time for embroidery and lace-making. They forget the crafts which once gave their clothes so much individuality.

▲ All Japanese ladies once wore silk kimonos and huge pins in their hair. Now they wear clothes suitable for work in offices and factories.

Scottish tartans

Lace jabot

Velvet Montrose doublet

Kilt pin

Sporran

Lace cuffs

Kilt of Stewart dress tartan

Dirk

Tartan hose

Dress brogues

◄ The short kilt worn by the clansmen of Scottish highland families is now mainly seen as evening dress. After the 1745 rebellion, a law banned the tartan and by the time it was repealed many of the old patterns were lost. But in the 19th century there was a revival of interest in Scottish history. All the clans acquired their own tartan colour schemes. The early vegetables dyes could not be produced in large quantities, so a subtle mixture of colours was used. Local dyestuffs led to local tartans. They only later became the property of particular clans.

The kilt is a practical garment in the rough damp terrain of the mountains. The sporran or pouch takes the place of pockets.

▲ The Stewart hunting tartan is typical in using darker colours for camouflage. The first clan tartans may have been for hunting.

▲ This is the dress Stewart tartan as worn by the man on the left. Many of the dress tartans have a white background.

▲ This black and white Erskine tartan is worn for mourning. Many other patterns are hundreds of years old but this is a modern design.

The evolution of the three piece suit

1468　1616

Barbarians in trousers

Trousers have been worn in central Asia for thousands of years both by women and men. Fierce tribes in full floppy trousers harassed the eastern frontiers of the Roman Empire. To the Romans these people were barbarians and a law was passed making trousers illegal for Roman citizens.

The tribes who overran Europe in the tenth century also wore warm leggings. Later, they adopted clothes of Roman origin. A mediaeval lord wore leggings of chain mail for battle, but in peace-time he wore a long robe. Only the peasant was seen outdoors in his underwear, known as braies or breeches.

There was a dramatic change in male fashions in the late 15th century. Instead of a long gown, a man wore a short tunic called a pourpoint. It was tied with laces, or points, to the tops of his woollen hose. These stockings were similar in shape to modern tights.

A practical uniform

The modern suit took another 300 years to evolve from this basic shape. But in spite of many changes of style, men's clothes always stressed the division of torso from legs. Women's clothes usually pretended they had no legs.

Until the end of the 17th century fashion was set by the royal courts, with the emphasis on decorative clothes. Gradually, court life became less important and country gentlemen set the pace. They were more interested in clothes which were practical.

The French Revolution coincided with the rise of vast industrial cities. Middle class men adopted a smart version of peasant trousers. With the once royal jacket and waistcoat they made up the three piece suit, a uniform for office workers in grey cities.

▲ These Muslim horsemen are wearing an early form of the coat which was worn in many areas of Asia. It reached to below the knees and usually had three-quarter length sleeves. It was open at the front and often split at the back for riding.

▶ 1680. After the Fire of London in 1666 Charles II tried to persuade the English to dress more soberly. He adopted the so-called "Persian vest" and wore a simple black version of it with sleeves short enough to show lace at the cuffs. The style was soon taken up by courtiers throughout Europe, but soon became more elaborate and highly-decorated.

1748. From 1700, clothes became simpler. On the battlefield and in the court a gentleman wanted clothes suitable for riding. Coat skirts were buttoned back and wigs became neater, usually tied into a queue with a satin bow.

▲ 1468. The pourpoint, with its padded shoulders and fur trimmings, belongs to one of the most fashion conscious periods in history. The long pointed shoes came from Poland and were called poulains. With the short pourpoint they drew attention to a man's legs.

1616. By now the tunic was lined and given front fastenings. It was known as a doublet because of the double thickness of cloth. The short trousers underneath were now called hose and what had been hose were now stockings. Blunt toed shoes were worn and a padded belly was considered manly. The short trunk hose were swollen with bran or rags.

The history of the collar and tie

The first ruff is said to have hidden a scar on the neck of the French King Henri II. Since then, neckwear has been an important sign of a man's status. Cravats and steinkirks were made of lace, so only the rich could afford them. In the early 19th century, men spent hours each day arranging their stocks. Even today, there are places where a man is not allowed without a tie.

▲ Ruffs were made of linen or lace. They were starched or held on wire frames.

1680  **1748**

1802  **1908**

▲ An 18th century sailor wearing trousers. Trousers were worn by working men in the last half of the 18th century and particularly by the mobs who overthrew the aristocracy of France. At the end of the century they were adopted by men of fashion.

▶ **1802.** The 19th century was the first age of urban fashion. The dandy's clothes were simple and plain coloured but beautifully cut. His elegance was lost as suits became dark and uniform.

1908. As the 19th century progressed, the myth arose that men were not interested in their appearance. By the turn of the 20th century even people whose jobs were dirty owned a "Sunday suit". Often, it lived from Monday to Saturday in the pawnshop. Not until the 1960s, when many 19th century values were overthrown, did colour and variety begin to return to men's clothes. But the three-piece suit is still firmly entrenched.

▲ The cravat became fashionable around 1660. The finest lace was often used.

▲ The steinkirk, named after a battle in 1692 when officers had to dress in a hurry.

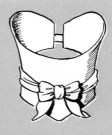

▲ The early 19th century stock led to the bow tie with a stiff detachable collar.

▲ Modern ties date from 1900. Only since 1945 have shirts had sewn-on collars.

Spot the worker

▶ These Buddhist monks wear the same flowing robes that have appeared on statues since the time of Buddha. Saffron yellow is their holy colour. The shaved head is a sign of submission in many religions. Christian monks sometimes have a shaved crown, which is called a tonsure.

▼ A Roman Catholic priest celebrates mass in vestments which are based on the everyday clothes of a Roman 1,500 years ago. The maniple was a towel carried by servants at banquets. The chasuble was originally a warm cloak with a head-hole like a poncho.

Protection and recognition

Many people wear special clothes when they are at work. The function of these clothes varies with the job. Some are designed to protect the body from dangerous conditions, like the helmets of miners and builders. Others only prevent the clothes underneath from getting dirty, such as the aprons and overalls of chemists, butchers and mechanics.

Uniforms are used for many jobs and have many advantages. A policeman can be recognised at once because of his uniform. It inspires respect by being dignified but slightly old fashioned. A helmet or cap partly hides the face. People pay more attention to the uniform than to the individual who wears it, so a policeman's military style clothes make his job easier.

Vestments for Catholic Mass

Stole

Chasuble

Maniple

Alb

▲ This man's job is to guide the planes in to land. A fluorescent jacket ensures that he is seen by the pilot.

Working clothes with a history

It would be useful if a doctor were as easy to recognise as a policeman. But the medical profession has no uniform. Doctors, like bankers, wear sober, formal clothes because they make people more ready to trust them. Casual clothes might suggest a casual attitude to the health of the patient.

Orchestral conductors and musicians wear the formal black evening dress of the late 19th century. It has become a uniform for the concert hall and a link with the golden age of music.

Religious clothes also change very slowly. Nuns wear the black habits of mediaeval widows. Many new religious orders were founded at that time. But they are working clothes and lately have been modernized for the benefit of nuns who nurse or teach.

▲ These peasants were painted in the 15th century and the artist has made them look far too clean. They wear no special clothes for work, but the man wears a bib to carry the seed. Aprons appear in the vast majority of peasant costumes.

◀ The pilot's uniform is similar to that of an airforce officer. At first airlines recruited most of their pilots from the services.

Airline staff and crew are provided with special uniforms. So are the ground staff who keep the plane in good mechanical order. Some airlines base their uniforms on national costume, but most prefer an efficient semi-military style.

▲ The steward and stewardess serve passengers with drinks and food in flight. But unlike waiters and waitresses on the ground, they have a smart modern-looking uniform. It looks efficient and they can be easily recognised.

Clothes for protection

▲ A reinforced helmet is worn by many manual workers.

▲ This mask protects its wearer from dust and fumes.

▲ Earmuffs are worn in noisy conditions.

▲ Various types of glove are made to give protection to the hands.

▲ Watertight thigh-length boots are worn by fishermen.

Changes of temperature

Unlike many other animals, man is not able to tolerate great changes of body temperature. If he is to live or work in very hot or cold places, he needs the protection of clothes.

One of the best ways of keeping an even temperature is to trap a layer of air between the folds of a loose garment. This principle is used by the people of the Sahara to keep cool. The same principle is also followed by tramps who stuff their clothes with sheets of newspaper to keep warm at night. The air trapped between the layers of paper stops the body's warmth escaping.

Danger from noise

Many sorts of protective clothing are designed to help people do jobs which would otherwise be dangerous. Ear guards have to be worn in some factories because of the high noise level. Continuous loud noise can permanently damage the hearing. It can also lead to accidents because it affects a person's ability to concentrate.

▶ Tuareg nomads in the Sahara wear loose robes and shield their faces from the sun and sand with a *taguelmoust*. This is a piece of cloth 6 m. (20 ft) long.

▼ The face mask, gloves and overall worn by the surgeon and staff of an operating theatre all help to keep the patient safe from germs.

Seeing and being seen

There are many sorts of protective covering to help people to see and be seen. Luminous orange jackets help prevent accidents to workmen on roads by making them easily visible.

Goggles are used to protect their wearers from dangers to the eye. A motorcyclist shields his eyes against flying grit. A welder using an oxy-acetylene flame needs protection from the glare and from sparks which may be as hot as 2,500°C.

For hundreds of years most Muslim women hid from men by veiling their faces. But Tuareg women, who are Muslims, have no veils while the men always cover their faces in public, even when eating or drinking.

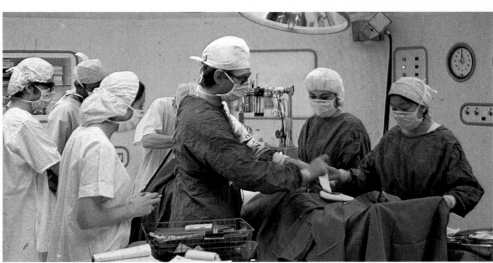

Cutaway of an integrated thermal micrometeoroid spacesuit

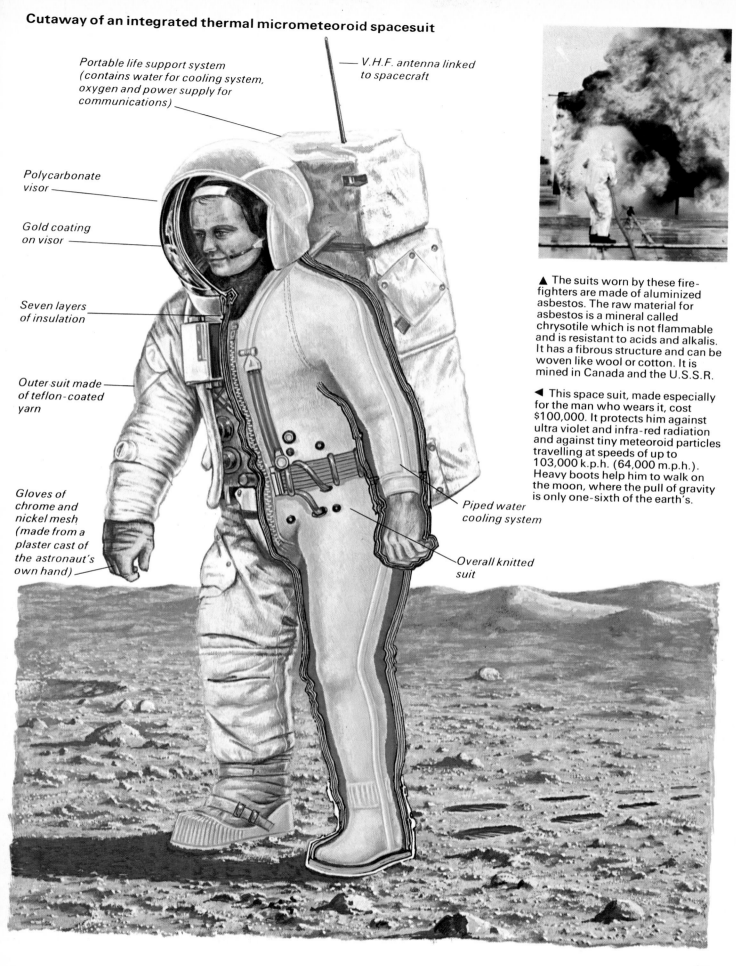

Portable life support system (contains water for cooling system, oxygen and power supply for communications)

V.H.F. antenna linked to spacecraft

Polycarbonate visor

Gold coating on visor

Seven layers of insulation

Outer suit made of teflon-coated yarn

Gloves of chrome and nickel mesh (made from a plaster cast of the astronaut's own hand)

Piped water cooling system

Overall knitted suit

▲ The suits worn by these fire-fighters are made of aluminized asbestos. The raw material for asbestos is a mineral called chrysotile which is not flammable and is resistant to acids and alkalis. It has a fibrous structure and can be woven like wool or cotton. It is mined in Canada and the U.S.S.R.

◄ This space suit, made especially for the man who wears it, cost $100,000. It protects him against ultra violet and infra-red radiation and against tiny meteoroid particles travelling at speeds of up to 103,000 k.p.h. (64,000 m.p.h.). Heavy boots help him to walk on the moon, where the pull of gravity is only one-sixth of the earth's.

Dressed to kill armour and uniforms

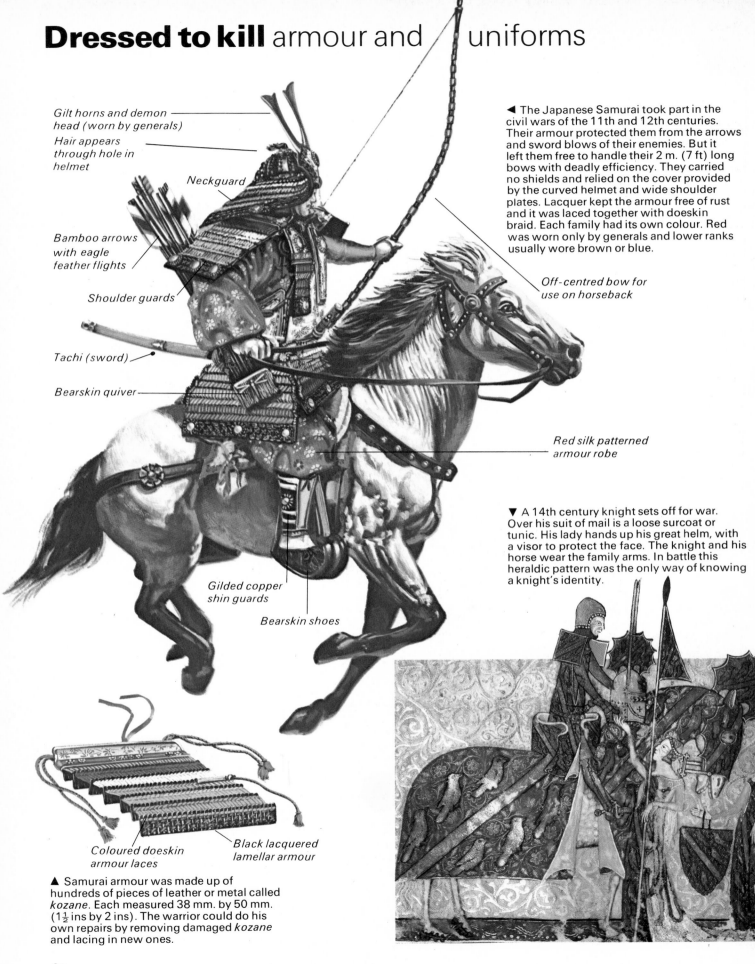

Gilt horns and demon head (worn by generals)

Hair appears through hole in helmet

Neckguard

Bamboo arrows with eagle feather flights

Shoulder guards

Tachi (sword)

Bearskin quiver

Gilded copper shin guards

Bearskin shoes

Coloured doeskin armour laces

Black lacquered lamellar armour

Red silk patterned armour robe

Off-centred bow for use on horseback

◄ The Japanese Samurai took part in the civil wars of the 11th and 12th centuries. Their armour protected them from the arrows and sword blows of their enemies. But it left them free to handle their 2 m. (7 ft) long bows with deadly efficiency. They carried no shields and relied on the cover provided by the curved helmet and wide shoulder plates. Lacquer kept the armour free of rust and it was laced together with doeskin braid. Each family had its own colour. Red was worn only by generals and lower ranks usually wore brown or blue.

▼ A 14th century knight sets off for war. Over his suit of mail is a loose surcoat or tunic. His lady hands up his great helm, with a visor to protect the face. The knight and his horse wear the family arms. In battle this heraldic pattern was the only way of knowing a knight's identity.

▲ Samurai armour was made up of hundreds of pieces of leather or metal called *kozane*. Each measured 38 mm. by 50 mm. (1½ ins by 2 ins). The warrior could do his own repairs by removing damaged *kozane* and lacing in new ones.

Battle dress

Fighting has always been one of man's principle occupations. The main use of clothes in battle is for protection. Leather, bronze and iron have all been used to make armour.

An army's morale is also important. Fine clothes make men proud and confident. So some of the most splendid costumes ever designed have been for war.

Uniforms did not become common until the 18th century, when armies were raised nationally. Some earlier troops had worn a cross or sash of a particular colour to identify them. Like uniforms these had encouraged a sense of unity. Medals and badges of rank are more noticeable when all soldiers are dressed alike.

Fashion also affects military dress. So many expensive periwigs were lost in early 18th century battles that officers adopted smaller wigs. Ceremonial dress often changes slowly. The Swiss Guard at the Vatican still wears a uniform designed by Raphael in the 16th century.

▼ The modern fighting man often wears camouflage. Steel helmets and strong boots protect the head and feet. But the rest of the khaki or khaki and green dress is designed to conceal him, especially from the air.

▶ This is the parade ground uniform of a sergeant of Napoleon's Imperial Guard of Grenadiers, who went with him on all his campaigns but were seldom used in action. Their purpose was to add lustre to an Empire which lasted from 1804 to 1815. The uniform was designed for splendour rather than military efficiency.

Imperial Eagle

Imperial Eagle on Shako plate

White straps supporting sword and ammunition pouch

Gold on red stripe above cuff

Musket weighing 4 kgs. (9 lbs.)

Chevron of ten years' service

Wool gaiters for winter use

Leaders

Clothes of authority

Kings, emperors and chiefs have usually worn special clothes to proclaim their authority. The clothes of leaders are not necessarily practical or easy to move in, though they may have been practical at first. They almost always include rare and precious materials and often record the important part early rulers played in the religious life of their people. The function of these clothes is to inspire awe and respect and to show off a nation's wealth and pride.

The Mandan Indians of North Dakota saw their chief as a supreme hunter. Their lives depended on the successful pursuit of food supplies. His ermine trimmings and magnificent cascade of feathers are typical of the deliberate luxury to be found in most leaders' clothes. His men went naked or with a loin-cloth, and with a single feather in their hair.

Coronation robes

During the coronation of Britain's Queen Elizabeth II in 1953 she was presented with a sword and spurs, for she too is descended from warriors.

The coronation robes include an imperial mantle shaped like a bishop's cope to represent her leadership of the Church of England. The crown used for the ceremony is based on the one made for St Edward, the king who built Westminster Abbey in the eleventh century.

▲ The Mandan Chief, Four Bears, is dressed as a warrior and hunter. On his tunic is an open palm to show that he has killed in hand-to-hand combat. The hair of other victims makes a fringe for his sleeves. He also wears buffalo horns, eagle feathers and a necklace of 50 grizzly bear claws.

◄ Queen Elizabeth II wears her most comfortable clothes to watch horse jumping. Modern leaders are expected to live an ordinary life when they are not on duty.

► Mao-tse tung has been one of the world's most powerful leaders for a quarter of a century. His revolution in China was based on a belief in sharing and equality. So he dresses to look as much like his people as possible, in working clothes.

▶ The Imperial dragon robe was worn by the Emperors of China until the revolution of 1912. The silk was dyed a special yellow, which could be used only by the Emperor and his heir. The embroidered pictures represent the earthly and divine powers of the Chinese ruler.

▼ The dragon in the centre is a sign of fertility. It clutches in its claw the flaming pearl of all knowledge and power. The dragon contains the lucky number nine. Parts of its body reminded the Chinese of nine other creatures including the snake and the stag.

▼ The twelve Imperial symbols are in four main groups which together sum up the earthly and divine powers of the Emperor.
    Sacrifices were made to the sun, moon, heaven and earth:
(1) The sun. (2) The moon. (3) The seven stars of the Great Dipper (heaven). (4) A mountain (earth). The power of nature is shown by:
(5) The paired dragons. (6) The pheasant.
The Emperor's power to judge and punish are contained in:
(7) The Fu sign. (8) The axe. Last are the four elements which were thought to make up life: (9) Bronze cups (metal). (10) Water weed (water). (11) Fire. (12) Millet seed (grain).

A means of protest

▼ This picture shows the kind of contrast that led to the French Revolution in 1789. The rich had money to waste on extravagant clothes. The poor often had not enough to eat. They were called *sansculottes* because they wore trousers, not breeches.

Proud citizens of the new republic dressed in red, white and blue, with tricolour cockades in their hats. Some French aristocrats were guillotined for refusing to wear the tricolour.

The man wears a Phrygian cap, or cap of liberty. It dates from biblical times and was also worn by the elected Duke of Venice, the Doge. He was a tyrant but his cap showed that the city was free from foreign rulers.

▶ The long thick robes worn by the Russian boyars, or nobles, in the 16th century were very different from western European fashions of the same period. The Tsar of Russia sent ambassadors to France and England, but the life of his people had not changed since the Middle Ages. The boyars were all bearded and often wore clothes made from the skins of wild bears.

Ungodly excesses

There are special clothes for leaders and uniforms for those who serve them. So rebels often express their protest through the things they wear.

In 17th century England, rich clothes and long curly hair were in fashion at Charles I's court. To the Puritans these were ungodly excesses. They were known as Roundheads because of their short cropped hair and they wore simple dark clothes to demonstrate their strong religious beliefs.

A simple way of life

The American hippy in the 1960s was opposed to a society ruled by money. His protest was against war, pollution and the anonymous life of big cities. The young men drafted for compulsory military service had to wear their hair in a severe crew cut so the hippy let his hair grow long and was usually bearded.

Many folk influences coloured hippy clothes. There were the beads and fringes of American Indians, African kaftans and Indian shirts and skirts. While the mini-skirt was becoming popular with other Americans, the hippy girl always wore a long flowing dress.

These clothes expressed a desire for a return to a way of life that was both simpler and more colourful. Like other famous rebels, the hippy believed that the only contented people are those who do creative work with their hands.

◀ Tsar Peter the Great decided to bring his people into line with Western ideas of civilisation. He ordered his boyars to wear French and German clothes and made them shave off their beards. He built the new city of St. Petersburg in the French style and French became the main language of the Russian court.

▶ Leo Tolstoy was one of Russia's greatest writers. He was the owner of a large estate but wanted to give his peasants their freedom. He wore peasant clothes and worked beside them in the fields. His beard also showed his lack of sympathy with the French-speaking ruling class.

▼ Giuseppe Garibaldi was one of the men who freed Italy from the Austrians in 1870. His red shirt was already part of his legend. It came from a batch of shirts made for slaughterhouse workers. They were coloured red to hide the blood. For Garibaldi's "Thousand" this shirt became a proud uniform.

▲ Ghandi's simple white clothing was part of his protest against British rule in India. He knew that his near nakedness embarrassed his enemies. By contrast the Aga Khan, leader of millions of Muslims, dressed and lived the life of a wealthy European.

Clothes for special occasions

▼ This is a Gcaleka initiation ceremony in the Transkei in South Africa. The young men celebrate their new manhood with dances. Each initiate wears a palm leaf skirt and a headdress which hides the face. The white clay on his body is decorated with spots to imitate the leopard, which is the emblem of the tribe.

Gcaleka initiation ceremony

Childhood ceremonies

At all the important stages of life there are ceremonies which involve the use of special clothes. The 16th century baby was wrapped in an ample white chrisom-cloth at christening. It took its name from the chrism oil used to annoint the child. High-born babies were also wrapped in luxurious mantles.

When Queen Elizabeth I was christened in 1533 she wore a mantle of purple velvet. It had a long train, edged with fur, which it took three people to carry. Shortly before 1800 white christening dresses came into use, often made of silk, satin or lace.

In many countries there are initiation ceremonies to mark the end of childhood. The young people often have to live away from their families for several weeks and the sexes are kept apart.

Protection from evil spirits

For their initiation ceremony, the girls of the Tukuna tribe are painted with red Urucu dye and decked with beads, necklaces and tassels. Their heads and faces are hidden by crowns of dazzling macaw feathers. Men dance around them disguised as girls or animals. Then the women pluck out the girls' hair. They are made to look entirely different so that evil spirits will not recognise them.

Weddings and funerals

White did not become the rule for European wedding dresses until the 19th century. Before that the bride wore her best clothes, but they could be of any colour.

Sherpa brides in Nepal still prefer to marry in their oldest clothes because they leave them behind when they go to live with their husbands.

White is the colour Europeans associate with the purity of the bride. But in China it was the colour worn at funerals and red was used for weddings.

White is also used for mourning in Zaire, where widows used to daub their faces with white clay. This custom was a disguise against evil spirits like the masks worn for initiation ceremonies. The bride's veil was originally worn for the same reason.

▲ This wedding picture from Thailand shows how European ceremonial clothes have spread around the world. Asian brides have only recently worn white. But the linking of the couple's heads with a white silk cord is an old part of the Thai wedding ceremony.

▼ At President Kennedy's funeral his widow and brothers wore black. The heavy veil was usual in 19th century mourning but is now seen only at state funerals. Men also used to tie long bands of crape to their hats, which trailed behind them. But the wearing of special clothes for mourning is becoming less and less common.

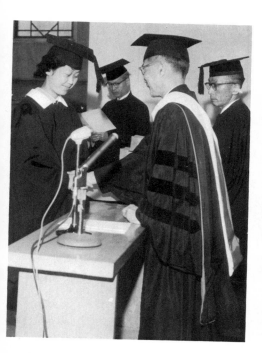

▲ Students at an American-style university in Japan are taking part in a graduation ceremony. The gown and mortar board evolved from clothes worn by educated Europeans in the 1500s. They are now worn at universities in all five continents.

Sportswear and the new equality

▲ No riding costume could be more impractical than this splendid dress worn by Princess Isabella de Bourbon in the 17th century. Now women ride in the same clothes as men.

Early clothes for sport

Modern sports clothes tend to be as functional as possible. They are designed to allow maximum freedom of movement, while giving whatever protection is needed. But for centuries games were played in clothes which look far from comfortable to modern eyes.

Professional sport has helped to make clothes easier to move in. Until 100 years ago Europeans played football in long trousers and even in hats. The game was also very confusing until teams started to wear different coloured shirts to identify them.

Shorts were first worn in the 1880s but they were very baggy in cut. It was another 20 years before they were short enough to uncover the knee. The development of special boots also helped to speed up the game.

▲ Mrs Bloomer tried to persuade women to wear pantaloons in the 1850s. But her costume was regarded as comical and indecent. Bloomers only became popular in the 1890s for the new sport of bicycling.

▼ Tennis clothes for women were long and restricting until the 1920s. Competitive players like Suzanne Lenglen realised how much their game would be improved by shorter skirts. But the general change was slow.

Swimming costumes

Even clothes for the open air are affected by the conflicting pull of tradition and fashion. Modern swimming costumes are a survival of 19th century ideas of decency. Until 1870 it was quite usual for men to swim naked, but within a few years it came to be seen as shocking. By the end of the century people on beaches wore as many clothes as they would in a city.

Women began to dress for a dip about 70 years earlier than men. Perhaps they realised how flattering a swimming costume could be. It usually followed the latest fashion and when waists were small there was even a rustless corset to wear in the water.

In the 1930s, for the first time in history, a sun-tan became attractive. It gave rise to the bikini, which reveals as much as it conceals and is very successful in arousing men's interest.

Men's everyday clothes often owe a great debt to sport. In 1800 the fashionable man wore the boots that are still worn by jockeys. The 19th century top hat, with its hard crown and narrow brim, was first used as an elegant crash helmet for hunting.

▲ Horse-racing was the first commercial sport. A jockey's clothes have not changed much in 200 years. The different coloured shirts indicate the horses' owners and help the spectator to tell one horse from another.

▼ Padded clothes and helmets protect the players in American football. Teams and individuals are identified by coloured shirts with numbers on them.

American football

Children's fashion past and present

Little adults

Children and adults have quite different ways of spending their time. But until the 19th century, there were no special clothes for children.

In the 16th century a boy was dwarfed by the padded doublet and trunk hose which were then in fashion. In the 1740s a girl was laced into a straight corset just like her mother's, and paniers made her skirt enormously wide. Clothes were chosen and paid for by parents.

A boy baby was kept tightly wrapped in swaddling clothes until he was ready to walk. Then he was dressed in skirts, just like his sister. At the age of five or six he was put into breeches.

The breeching ceremony was important to the whole family because so many children died before they reached this age. The eldest son was heir to his father's name and property. Once in breeches he was expected to behave like an adult.

Arranged marriages

One of the main functions of adult clothes is sexual attraction. To modern people it may seem strange that little girls were often dressed as fully grown women. But until the 19th century it was not usual for a girl to choose her own husband. It was her parents who decided whom she would marry. This is still the case in some Asian countries.

The marriage might be arranged when she was only seven or eight years old. So there was never a time when she was not seen as someone's future bride, and she was dressed accordingly.

Tough clothes

19th century parents understood that boys could have more fun in clothes that would stand rough wear. The sailor suit was neat and practical and was popular at a time of great colonial expansion.

Blue denim jeans are the modern equivalent. They were worn by settlers, ranch hands and gold prospectors in America in the last century. The pockets and seams were strengthened with metal rivets.

In the 1960s they became the uniform of a whole generation and were the first children's fashion to be seized on by adults.

▲ An Italian prince of the 17th century in swaddling clothes. People swaddled babies because they believed this would help them grow tall and straight. There is still some swaddling in South America.

▼ The late 19th century nanny (1) was paid to look after the children of wealthy parents. Her formal uniform showed that she was a servant and not a member of the family, but she ruled the children's lives.

▲ Italian schoolboys wear a simple uniform of white overall and blue bow (2). The girls' uniform is very similar. A Victorian boy (4) wore skirts until he was breeched at the age of five or six.

▲ A 17th century French peasant boy (3) was much freer in his clothes than a rich boy. His parents could never afford shoes so his bare feet were as hard as leather. Rags and dirt did not worry him so long as he had enough to eat.

▼ Two children (5 and 6) in French fashions around 1700. The lace fontange on the girl's head was named after a favourite of Louis XIV. The stiffly-boned bodice of the dress and its long train made energetic games impossible. The Chinese boy (7) is of the same period. He is obviously happy riding his toy horse and not hampered by wearing clothes like his father's.

▼ Young people today (11 and 12) wear clothes which never spoil their fun. Girls can be as active as boys now that T-shirts and jeans can be worn by anyone. A girl's school uniform (13) mixes male and female styles and often includes a tie in the school colours.

▼ A boy's clothes in 1800 were stylish but practical (8). His jacket is like his father's but with the tails cut off. The shirt is frilly by modern standards but then seemed very plain and unfussy.

▼ 19th century girls (9) had short skirts but even a child's legs could not be seen, so they wore thick stockings or long bloomers.

▼ Sailor suits (10) were very popular for both sexes, though the girls wore skirts with theirs. At this time many European powers had vast navies and were expanding their empires.

The entertainers costumes for theatre and dance

▲ The Kathakali dancers of southern India perform stories from Hindu legends. They are accompanied by a narrator and musicians. The female parts are played by men but it is the male characters who wear the more exotic costumes. Under their skirts there can be as many as 24 layers of petticoats. The shape of the skirt is like a 16th century farthingale.

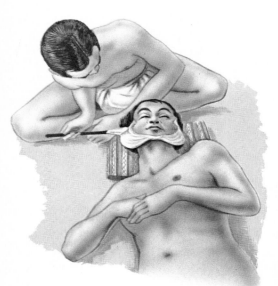

◄ The dancer's life is hard so he sleeps while his make-up is put on. It may take four hours and he wakes up a different character. The artist uses a bamboo twig and builds up the false chin with rice paste. Heroes wear green make-up, while villains have red beards or warts on their noses. The ground-stone colours are mixed with oil.

The origins of theatre

All forms of theatre began with religious ceremonies. Masks and weird costumes enabled priests to impersonate the spirits and gods who controlled earthly life. Music, dance and the singing or reciting of religious texts combined to create a spectacle.

At first these spectacles had no audience, for everyone was involved. In Africa and South America the division can still be blurred between religious festivals and entertainment.

Clothes for the character

In the West, theatre, films and television plays mainly show characters in everyday clothes. Their main function is to indicate to the audience the nature of the man or woman wearing them.

A trendy get-up has quite a different impact from one that is years out of date. An audience "reads" the difference without being aware of it. This saves the author time in describing the personalities.

Masks did the same job in Greek and Roman classical theatre. They dealt with character in a broad general way: Hero, Shepherd, Old Man. This enabled one actor to play more than one part in a play.

Modern costume

In the West, theatre has broken up into three areas: dance, opera and spoken drama. In ballet very free athletic movement is expected so the audience has learnt to "read" character from tiny hints in the brief costumes.

Opera still uses elaborate clothes, though the effect of richness is often obtained by simple means. Jewels may be made from bottle-tops or buttons; brocade and embroidery from painted patterns on cheap cloth.

There is a special costume problem for plays not set in the present day. Some designers and directors are excited by the chance to create a real historical atmosphere through period clothes. Others use modern dress to bring the audience into closer contact with the characters. But there is bound to be a conflict between today's clothes and the language of Shakespeare. Both bear the mark of a particular society at a particular time.

42

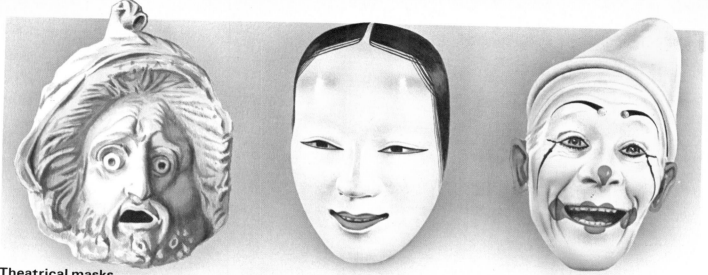

Theatrical masks

▲ The Greeks wore masks for tragedy and comedy. The strongly-drawn character and shape of the mouthpiece helped them to be seen and heard clearly in the huge outdoor amphitheatre.

▲ The masks in Japanese "Noh" plays are worn by men playing female roles. The simple design of the features allows the performer to vary the mood with subtle movement and tone of voice.

▲ The clown is an anarchist. He wants to destroy his audience's normal reaction to life. His wild make-up, wig and clothes make it possible to laugh at the cruel things which happen to him.

▲ David Bowie on stage. Make-up and costume often play an important part in a pop star s act. He, too, wants to destroy ordinary ways of looking at the world. He even uses a woman's lipstick and eye-shadow to challenge the distinction between male and female.

◄ The clothes and shoes worn for classical ballet are instantly recognisable. Their main purpose is to give the dancer freedom of movement. The ballerina has block-toed shoes to support her in the pointwork and a skirt so short that it shocked 19th century prudes. The male dancer is given flexibility by his light knitted tights.

43

Projects experiment with clothes

Make and wear a sari

The loose, untailored clothes worn by tradition in many parts of the world feel very different from western clothes. You can find out how different by making a sari (worn by Indian women) or a sarong (worn by men in Malaysia). These clothes have no buttons, belts or zips so you will find that you have to move carefully in them.

Most saris are made of very lightweight cloth but you can reproduce the shape with old curtains or sheets. Take one double bed sheet. (But be sure that it is never going to be needed again as a sheet.) Fold it in two along its length and cut from end to end. This will give you two pieces each about 1 m. × 2 m. (3 ft × 6 ft). Repair any torn areas and hem the cut edges to prevent fraying. Sew the two pieces together end to end. You will than have a single strip about 4 m. long (14 ft).

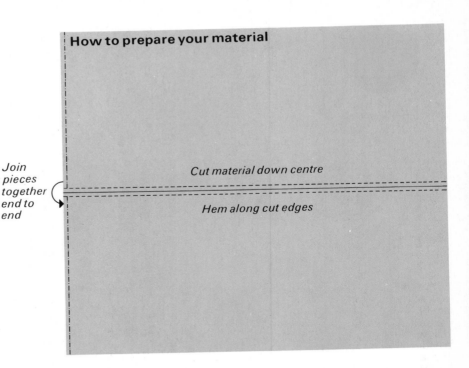

How to prepare your material

Join pieces together end to end

Cut material down centre

Hem along cut edges

How to put on the sari

▲ A sari is usually worn over a kind of T-shirt that leaves the midriff bare, with a petticoat from waist to ankle. But try it over jeans or pyjama trousers. Tuck one end into the waistband of your jeans. Let the width drop to your ankles. Wrap the length around you.

▼ When you come back to where you started and have made a skirt, gather three pleats. Tuck them into the waistband beside the first tuck. The skirt should be pulled fairly tight otherwise it will tend to droop.

▲ Take the remainder of the sari across your chest and under your left armpit. Then bring it around your back and under your right armpit.

▼ Finally, bring the end of the sari across your chest and over your left shoulder. If you keep your left arm up it will now make a kind of sleeve. Your right arm is quite free. If you are left handed reverse all these instructions.

Make a Malaysian sarong

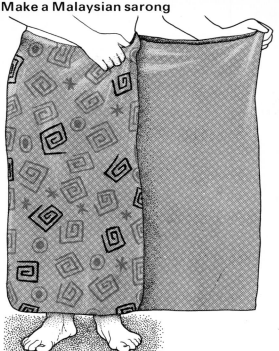

▲ A Malay sarong uses only half of a double bed sheet. Cut it lengthways as for a sari. Hem the cut edges. Then sew the two ends together so that they make a wide loop or tube of cloth. In Malaysia, the sarong is often worn over flimsy trousers so wear your pyjamas. A piece of curtain 1 m. × 2 m. (3 ft × 7 ft approx.) could also be used.

▲ To put on a sarong you first step into the middle of the tube. Pull the top edge of the cloth out to your left as far as you can reach. Hold it there and put your right hand on your left hip. Bring the cloth in your left hand over towards your right hip. Remove your right hand and tuck the end of the sarong into itself.

Fabric printing

Colourful fabric designs can be made with nothing more than a packet of dye, a sharp knife and a potato. Slice a large potato in half. Cut away the flesh so that the pattern you want stands out. Keep it simple. The way you space it on the cloth will make it look interesting. Read the instructions on the dye packet very carefully. Wear old clothes and put thick layers of newspaper under the cloth. Put a little dye on your potato and press onto the cloth.

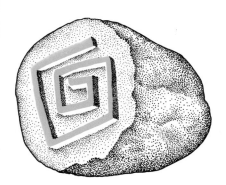

▲ This pattern was cut out and used to decorate the sarong on the left.

Fashion surveys

Test the effect of fashion by making a survey of what people are wearing. You need a strong notebook, a pencil and a little patience. Start with a fashion which is easy to spot. I put people into four age groups and looked for platform soled shoes, making a tick for each pair I saw. Your surveys could count men in suits, women in trousers, beards or the number of people in the latest fashionable colour.

Working with a friend you can conduct a more complex survey, such as types of hat. One person notes all the hats which are part of a uniform (police helmets, school cap etc.), or strictly for protection (crash helmets). The other notes hats that are purely for pleasure. Both of you take note of the age ranges.

Don't be surprised if your results are quite different from the fashion trends reported in newspapers. Many fashions never really catch on. But expect your survey to be affected if you make your count near a school, old people's home or factory. Each will provide an unusual concentration of one sort of clothes.

Platform-soled shoes survey

	0-15	15-30	30-45	Over 45	
Quantity seen	✓✓	✓✓✓✓✓ ✓✓✓✓✓ ✓✓✓✓✓ ✓✓✓	✓✓✓		
TOTALS	2	18	3	0	23

Hats survey

	0-15	15-30	30-45	Over 45	
Hats as a uniform or protective	✓✓✓	✓✓	✓✓✓✓✓ ✓✓✓		
TOTALS	3	2	8	0	13
Hats for pleasure		✓✓✓✓✓ ✓		✓✓✓✓ ✓	
TOTALS	0	5	1	5	11

Reference and glossary

How to study historical costume

Most good local museums have some examples of costumes from other periods of history. Collections of accessories such as hats, purses and shoes are even more common. In England the museums which have good permanent costume sections are the following:

The Victoria and Albert Museum, London (also for jewellery and lace)

Geffrye Museum, London

The Museum of Costume, Bath

Gallery of English Costume, Manchester

The Castle Museum, York (also for military costume)

The British Museum has collections of sculpture, painted vases etc. which give good information on the ancient costumes of Rome, Greece, Egypt and Assyria. There are also splendid displays of jewellery.

The Museum of Mankind shows a changing selection of exhibits. They give an impression of the lives of societies not influenced by Western Europe and sometimes include costumes and masks.

For uniforms, the National Army Museum, National Maritime Museum and the Imperial War Museum in London are very useful.

Many old churches in England have effigies and brasses which show period costume. They mainly cover the period between the 11th and 16th centuries.

Paintings and photographs

You can buy Edwardian pin-up cards of famous actresses and beauties. But the photo albums of grandparents and aunts will show you best what people were wearing quite recently and how different they were from today's clothes.

Antique shops often have framed fashion plates, mainly of 19th century costumes. These are expensive to buy but it costs nothing to look at them. Porcelain figures also give a good view of costume.

Experts can often discover the exact year in which a picture was painted by the clothes worn by the subjects. All over the country there are old houses which are open to the public on certain days and most of these contain old portraits. Public art galleries are very good places to study historical costume, and they all sell postcard reproductions which are not expensive.

Try collecting one or two cards showing the costumes of each century since 1400. When you have begun to recognize the general outline of the clothes of one period, start collecting postcards of that period only. The variations worked on a particular style can be very interesting.

Books to read

General

A Concise History of Costume by James Laver (Thames and Hudson)

Fashion through Fashion Plates by Doris Langley Moore (Ward Lock)

Fashion by Ludmilla Kybalova (Paul Hamlyn)

Fashion by Mila Contini (Paul Hamlyn)

A Dictionary of English Fashion by C. Willett Cunnington (A. & C. Black)

A Handbook of English Costume (5 books covering each century from the Middle Ages to the 19th century) by C. W. Cunnington (Faber)

English Costume (Seven books: Middle Ages to 19th century) by Iris Brooke (A. & C. Black)

Special subjects

Corsets and Crinolines by Norah Waugh

Jewellery Hamlyn all colour Paperbacks

National Costume Hamlyn all colour Paperbacks

History of Make-up by Maggie Angeloglou (Studio Vista)

Ancient Greek, Roman and Byzantine Costume by Mary G. Houston (A. & C. Black)

Flowering of the Middle Ages (Thames and Hudson)

Punch History of Manners and Modes by Alison Adburgham (Hutchinson)

Costume Cavalcade by Henry Harald Hansen (Eyre Methuen)

English Children's Costume (Since 1775) by Iris Brooke (A. & C. Black)

Royal Courts of Fashion by Norman Hartnell (Cassell)

African Elegance by Alice Mertens and Joan Broster (Macdonald)

Glossary

Breeches 18th century garment covering men's legs, buttoned or buckled at the knee.

Bustle Padding on a woman's bottom. Fashionable for the last 30 years of the 19th century.

Chiton Loose woollen or cotton draped clothing worn in Ancient Greece.

Cope Cloak worn by bishops. Usually with heavy embroidery, open down the front.

Crinoline Padding to widen skirts; at first using horsehair (in French 'crin'), from 1856 steel hoops.

Doublet 16th and 17th century jacket with front fastenings.

Farthingale The padded skirts worn by women in the 16th and 17th centuries.

Fontange Tall lace head-dress worn by fashionable ladies in the late 17th century.

Gin Cotton cleaning machine. Short for engine.

Habit Name given to the uniform of nuns and monks. Also used of riding clothes in the late 19th century.

Heddle A weaving device that raises some of the warp threads so as to make a path, or shed, for the weft.

Hose i) In the Middle Ages: Stockings and tights. ii) In the 16th century: short trousers, also called trunk hose.

Kilt Short skirt worn by men in Scotland. Fastened with a large pin like a safety pin. Also worn in Greece.

Kimono Loose coat-shaped dress, usually of light-weight cloth, worn in Japan by both sexes.

Mordant Any chemical substance used to make dye permanent.

Muslin Very fine cotton cloth, almost transparent.

Nylon The first synthetic fibre

Panniers Basket work used to extend 18th century skirts.

Pourpoint 15th century tunic, fastened at the back or under the arms.

Rayon The first man-made fibre.

Shuttle Contains the weft thread in weaving.

Tailoring Giving clothes their style by cutting cloth into shaped pieces and sewing them together.

Tunic Garment which covers the top of the body as far as the hips or longer. May or may not have sleeves.

Warp Threads which run through the length of woven cloth.

Weft Threads which run across the width of woven cloth.

Index

Illustration Credits

Key to the position of illustrations: (T) top, (C) centre, (B) bottom and combinations: (CL) centre left, (TR) top right.

Artists

Sackett Publishing Services Ltd.: 3 (L), 39
Michael Youens/Sackett Publishing Services Ltd.: 3 (R)
Eric Jewell Ass.: 4-5, 18-19
Dave Smith/Zip Art: 6-7
Tony Payne: 7 (TR), 10-11, 20-1, 28-9, 32-3, 42-3
Keith Ward/Zip Art: 8-9
Gwen Green/Sackett Publishing Services Ltd.: 12-13, 19 (B), 22-3, 26-7, 34-5, 36, 40-1
Shirley Bellwood/B. J. Kearley Ltd.: 14-15, 24-5 (B)
Glen Mitchell/Zip Art: 16-17
Kathy Wyatt: 24-5 (T)
Brian Lebrani/Zip Art: 30-1
Ray Burrows & Corinne Clarke: 44-5

Photographs

Aerofilms Ltd.: 13 (L)
British Museum/photo: John Freeman 16 (R)
Canada House: 3
Coloursport: 39
Cooper Bridgeman: 30
Courtaulds Limited: 18
Crown Copyright: 31
Duke of Bedford: 8
Glaxo: 28 (B)
Sonia Halliday: 24
Robert Harding: 28 (T)
Michael Holford: 5 (T), 13 (R)
Victor Kennett: 4 (L), 5 (B), 42
Keystone Press: 32 (L & R), 37 (BR)
Mansell Collection: 7, 10, 14, 25, 35 (TL & BL), 38 (R), 40
Marks & Spencer: 20, 21
National Gallery: 16 (L)
Pictor: 37 (T)
Popperfoto: 37 (BL)
Prado: 38 (T)
Radio Times Hulton Picture Library: 35 (TR & BR), 38 (B)
Starr-Duffy: 43 (L)
J. Stevens: 43 (R)
T.B.A. Industrial Products: 29
United Nations: 22 (TL)
Victoria and Albert Museum: 9, 23 (T), 27, 33
Wilt Mellor Bromley Ltd.: 11